REMEMBRANCES

OF

TIMES OF MY LIFE

Rose Grosso

Dedication

I would like to dedicate this book to my loving parents, Catherine and Vincent Sarullo. Their love for each other and for our entire family nurtured me throughout my life.

My mother and I sitting in front of Hegney Place

I was born August 23, 1924 at 646 Hegney Place in the borough of the Bronx, New York City where I lived until I was ten years old. It was a plain house, three stories actually. We occupied the first floor which consisted of four rooms. It was a cold water flat. To keep warm we had this big stove in the kitchen which was also used for cooking.

We were a large family, eight to be exact – Grandma, Father, Mother, four older brothers and me. There was a big backyard where my father grew vegetables and tomatoes on one half and on the other half we could play. We had this little shed there which we played in when it rained.

Every fall my father bought grapes and he would make wine down in the cellar. We would all help. I enjoyed eating the grapes, I was too small to be much help.

There were railroad tracks across the street. At night

when they coupled up the freight trains they would bang so hard they would wake us up. It wasn't so bad in the winter – all the windows were closed.

We didn't have a radio at first and there was no television in those days, so we all sat around the table and played games. There was a lotto game and cards, and another game of racing horses. We always had a lot of fun.

Those were good times. There were bad times too. I remember when my father and my two older brothers had to go out working in the city. They had shoeshine boxes and they would shine shoes for money. I felt so bad for them, especially in the cold weather.

Summer time was the best time. We would be outside playing and Mom, Pop and Grandma would be sitting outside enjoying the fresh air. Then we all got ice cream or lemon ice. I remember it well.

I remember the times around election day. All the big

boys would gather all the wood they could find. They even took newsstands from candy stores. They would then make a big fire in the middle of the road and burn everything. Everyone stood around and watched the fire. Some of us kids would put a potato on a stick and roast it. They were so good.

We kids used to play outside. There was tag, jumping rope, roller skating, hopscotch – even playing school or house. When I was alone, when my friends were away, I always loved to play jacks. Occasionally when I was very young, I would put my kitten in my doll carriage and walk up and down the block.

I remember when I was little, my brothers and their friend would make carts. They were called skating carts. They were made from empty fruit crates and old roller skate wheels. The boxes were nailed to a long board that looked like a scooter. Roller skates were pulled apart and the wheels were put in the front and in the back of the board. Then they would have races up and down the block. They had a lot of fun. Sometimes I was given a ride in one. I would squeeze into the box -- and off we would go! It really was great fun.

The boys always played stick ball in the street. They didn't have to worry about cars, there weren't any coming through our block. There were very few around.

I do remember when I was little I would save two pennies so I could run around the corner to the candy store and buy a Hooton chocolate bar. The reason I liked them so much was that they were thick and lasted so long when I licked the chocolate.

We got our first radio in 1932, an Atwater Kent. As a little girl I loved to sing. I would go around the house singing songs I heard on the radio. My mother thought I was good, so she wrote to the Italian radio station she always

4

**This is me in my Communion Dress
with my Cousin Kitty**

listened to. When the man from the station came to our house to hear me sing, I just froze. I wouldn't open my mouth. My mother kept saying, "Sing for him, sing for him" to no avail. Maybe I could have made money for my family, made them rich. They sure could have used it. Times were tough.

I was surprised I was so shy, as I grew up with four older brothers. Guess I took after my father, he was a shy and a quiet man.

**My Mother and Father with
my brothers Gene, Salvator and Dominic**

Mother, Father and Grandmother

As a little girl I remember listening to my parents, who came from Sicily. They would talk in Italian about the time before I was born when my mother was a seamstress in Manhattan. My mother was a great seamstress. It was in "Hell's Kitchen" where my folks had this business. What they talked about was how the Mob called "The Black Hand" would go around to all the business owners and demand money. If you didn't pay up, bad things would happen to you or your family. These so called "Black Hand" mobsters originated in Sicily.

At this time, there were seven members in this family – Father, Mother, Grandmother and the four young boys. I guess it was about this time that my folks decided to close up shop and move away. That's when they bought the three story house at Hegney Place in the Bronx. They occupied the first floor, and the other two floors were rented out. It was supposed to help out as additional income for the family. My father was the only bread earner, although mother and the boys also did some work. However, my folks were soft-hearted people and they rented the flats to relatives who couldn't pay. I have no idea what they were charging for rent. It couldn't have been very much.

My Mother Catherine was born in Palermo, Sicily in 1890, she was the youngest of thirteen children. There were five boys and eight girls. Her father, my Grandfather whose name was Rosario, was a tobacconist and a chemist. He was a well respected man. Apparently the family was financially comfortable, because he left dowries for all the girls. The oldest son, Matthew, was in charge of distributing said dowries to his sisters upon their marriages. I never had the pleasure of knowing my Grandfather, he died in Sicily before my Grandmother and some of her children came to America. My Mother was fortunate, because she was able to go to school in Italy. Poorer families couldn't send their children to school, they were usually sent out to work.

When my Mother came over to America from Italy with members of her family, her mother, sisters and brothers, she was a young woman. She told us that she got so very sick crossing over on the ship. As a result she never liked to go into the water when we went to the beach. She never let any of us kids go in either. As a result, I never learned how to swim.

When I was young and living at Hegney Place, my Mother would go into New York City to the factories and pick up work to be done at home. Sometimes it was dresses or pillow cases or other sewing items. She also went to factories that made jewelry. There she got the material to make up necklaces and bracelets. You had to put the beads on thread or wire. Everything had to be done just right. We kids helped her with all this work. It was hard work. This was how my Mother supplemented my Father's income. We all chipped in and did our share.

My Father Vincent was born in Messina, Sicily in 1891. He had two older brothers. When he was a very young boy his mother died and his father later remarried. He didn't like his stepmother, she was too hard on the boys. At age eight he was sent to a ladies shoe factory as an apprentice. When his brother Joseph came to America with his wife Rosalie and their five children, my Father came with them. He was young and single. He never went to school. In later years when he married my Mother, she taught him to read and write in Italian.

Aunt Rosalie was my Mother's older sister, so I imagine that is how my Father got to know Mom. Two brothers married two sisters. Mom and Pop were married here in America, I believe it was about 1910.

I mentioned that my father was a shoemaker. He made the shoes from bottom to top, literally. He had to prepare the shoe last for the leather. He soaked the leather sole in water to soften it. I can't remember how he prepared the upper leather. I saw him make a hole in the sole with an awl. Then he had a special needle that was threaded with what looked like a thin strip of leather. It could have been a special kind of thread. Anyway, he sewed the upper leather to the sole, first making a hole in the upper leather also. He would then pull the needle through both holes and knot it. He continued to do this until the sole was completely sewed onto the upper leather. It was hard work and really tough on his fingers. I don't remember if he wore any kind of gloves. When he was finished with that part, he then made the holes for the shoelaces.

The finished product was a beautiful, soft leather

lady's shoe.

He used to repair my shoes when I got holes in them. Being that I used to love to play jump rope, I would wear out the soles. Many times my father would get very angry at me. I didn't tell him right away that I had holes in my shoes. I wore them right out through the inside of the shoe. That, of course, made it a tougher and longer repair job.

My Grandmother with one of the boys

My Grandmother's name was Francesca. She lived with us until she was ninety-three, she died in 1936. She was a small woman, but very strong and had all her teeth. She never ate fresh bread, she liked it a day old, and she cracked nuts with her teeth. She was never sick and always took care of us when my Mother was out. Her biggest problem was coping with arthritis. She did sewing for Mom, darning socks and whatever else needed repairing. I used to thread the needle for her, it was hard for her to see the tiny needle eye.

My Brothers - Salvator, Dominick, Gene and Frank

I would like to talk first about my brother Salvator. He was the second oldest of the four boys. He was a very talented young man. I remember when I was little he used to sit at the piano and play. He played by ear, he didn't have any notes in front of him. Also, he used to write music. He would play the notes and then put them down on paper. He also played the saxophone and the harmonica. Boy, I sure wish that I had his talent. Unfortunately, he couldn't proceed with his talent. He came down with lung disease. They called it pleurisy.

Also, I remember that we used to have chickens in our backyard, and a few rabbits. My brother Salvator had a pet chicken that he raised from a little chick. He would whistle to it and it would come running to him. He would do this everyday. When his chicken died a few years later, he refused to eat any chicken my Mother cooked. He never ate

My brother Salvator

chicken for the rest of his life.

He used to call me in when I was outside playing to cook him some spaghetti. He was six years older than me. I also fried him some eggs. He was a bit bossy. At one time, I got mad at him and kicked him in the leg. He told Mom and I got scolded.

My brother Dominick was prone to accidents. When he was a young boy he was down in the cellar chopping wood for the kitchen stove when he hit himself between the eyes with the ax. That was a close call, he could have hit his eye. He carried that scar the rest of his life. On another occasion he sprained his ankle when he jumped on a wine barrel that was sitting out in the yard.

My brother Gene as a teenager

My oldest brother Gene was so good to me. He would trim my hair and then brush it. He taught me how to dance and act like a little lady. He always got mad at me when I was little because I got dirty playing outside, especially my clothes.

My brother Frank was talented too. He played the banjo and the piano. He took many piano lessons. He started at Wurlitzer, then Steinway Hall and also at a practice room in Carnegie Hall. Unfortunately he had to give up the lessons because of lack of money.

My brother Frank

Aunts, Uncles and Cousins

When we lived at Hegney Place, my Aunt Nellie and her husband Uncle Dominick would come over to our house to settle their arguments. We kids used to call Uncle Dominick "Prince Albert." There was a can of tobacco called Prince Albert and Uncle Dominick looked and dressed like the man on the can of tobacco. When we saw them coming down the street we would run into the house and yell "the Prince Alberts are coming!" They looked so comical. The father was on one side, the mother on the other and their daughter Grace in the middle. Grace towered over them.

My aunt and uncle would accuse each other of trying to poison the other. She would say he was, and he would say she was. Sometimes we kids would stay inside and listen to them talking, always in Italian. After many such visits it became a bore, so we would go out and play. We really felt sorry for my cousin Grace, to have to live with them. It certainly wasn't a happy household.

Also I remember later on when I was walking to my junior high school and Grace was a senior there. She would be flanked on either side by her mother and father. Her parents wouldn't let her go by herself. They really were a sight to behold. I wondered if they thought someone would kidnap her.

My Cousin Grace, grown up, with my brothers

Salvator and Gene

Anyway, she did grow up to be a lovely young lady. She did some modeling work and taught me how to use makeup. Grace was a great pianist. I think she gave many recitals. Unfortunately she passed away many years ago.

My cousin Frances – we used to call her Kitty – lived near us. She lived in an apartment house on 149th Street with her younger brother Joseph. So it wasn't too far to walk to our house on Hegney Place. On Saturdays my brother Frank and I would go over to her house and help her clean. We dusted and polished all the furniture.

Joe had a parrot which they kept on a stand in the kitchen. Kitty didn't like the parrot. It bit her on the cheek once and many other times on her hand. The parrot didn't like her either. So whenever Kitty tried to clean the stand, it would bite her. One time she got so mad at it that she slapped it and it went flying across the room. Cousin Joe got mad at her for doing that, he loved his pet.

I know I never went near it when I was there. I was afraid of it. He was nasty.

Cousin Joe worked for an ice cream company. At the end of his day, if he had any ice cream left in the containers, he would bring it to us. We would all dig into the cans with a spoon, it was so good.

Kitty was very good to me. She used to pick me up on Fridays and take me to her place. I liked that a lot because I was able to take a bath. We didn't have a bathtub. We just had a "water closet" – a toilet – and had to go in the kitchen to wash up. During the week my Mother would put up a sheet by the stove and two basins of water so I could wash myself. So you can imagine how good a true bath felt to me. Frances was my Godmother at my confirmation.

Years later Joe moved out and took his parrot with him. Later on Kitty married Danny and they moved to Long Island.

Our Holidays, Outings and Vacations

Now when the holidays approach, I remember how we used to celebrate them as kids.

On Halloween, all the kids would buy a box of colored chalk at the candy store. Then we would chalk each other up and say "Halloween!" We not only chalked each other up, we would chalk up the sidewalk and the stoops. The worst part was when the boys would fill up a stocking with flour. They would go around and hit everyone with the the stockings. That really hurt. That's the way it was when I was a kid.

Thanksgiving was the time we dressed in costumes. We would go around ringing doorbells and asking "Anything for Thanksgiving?" We mostly got fruit or nuts, sometimes money. There was always a "Ragamuffin Parade." Everyone in the parade was dressed as clowns, hobos and others. I never marched in the parade, but I loved to watch them go by. It was fun for everyone. Today it is too commercialized. The grownups have taken over. It isn't the same anymore.

One year, I think when I was eight years old, I had a special Thanksgiving costume. I was supposed to be a chicken in a class play at school. My Mother was so happy to hear that. She went to the chicken market and asked if she could have all the feathers from the dead birds. They thought she was crazy! She got the feathers and she made me a chicken costume, sewing all the feathers onto gray material. Most of the feathers were gray. My Mother even made me a headpiece exactly like a chicken. I had yellow on my head and feet, just like the bird.

When the day came for the play, I walked into class in my chicken suit. The teacher and all of the kids were amazed. They couldn't believe it. All I did on stage was walk around and flap my arms like wings. That was my stage debut.

So of course I wore the chicken costume on Thanksgiving that year, going door to door asking "Anything for Thanksgiving?"

I remember that because Grandma lived with us at Hegney Place we celebrated all of the holidays there. My aunts and uncles and cousins would come over and then the women got busy cooking. We had this big kitchen and we all sat around the large round table to eat. There was plenty of food and also wine. We had a wine cellar, so one of my brothers would go down with a pitcher and get the wine out of the barrel. All he had to do was turn on the spigot and fill up the pitcher.

On one holiday when everyone was sitting down to eat, my Father asked my brother Frank to go down with the pitcher and fill it with wine. I think Frank was about nine or ten years old. He always had a bit of trouble turning the spigot off on the barrel, so what he used to do was drink the wine so it wouldn't spill on the floor. This happened every time he went down to refill the pitcher. By the third or fourth time he was woozy and couldn't climb the stairs. My Father kept calling him- "What's keeping you? Bring up the pitcher of wine." Finally some grownup went down and they found Frank slumped on the steps. He was drunk. They all got a big laugh out of this incident. Frank didn't touch another bit of wine for over ten years.

On one holiday, I think it was Thanksgiving, we were all sitting around the table eating, when my Mother said she wished her brother Mathew and his wife Amelia were there also. My cousin Dominick who had a car said, why don't we take a ride to Wrightstown and surprise them. So we gathered up the food in the tablecloth and put it in the car. Then we all piled in the car and rode off. We were ten people, kids sat on someone's lap. It was after midnight when we got there. My Aunt and Uncle were so very surprised and so happy to see us all.

I remember one Christmas Eve Grandma wanted to go to Midnight Mass, so my oldest brother, Gene, and the rest of us took her to Saint Rock's Church. When we got there, we weren't allowed to go into the church unless we had tickets. Imagine, you had to buy a ticket to go to Mass. It was horrible. Gene kept arguing with the man. Grandma is old, he said, she just wants to go into the church for Midnight Mass. It was no use, we were turned away. Needless to say we were all heart broken for Grandma. We never went back to that church again.

During the early years at Hegney Place I remember my Father and Mother and my brother Frank and I going to the Brooklyn Academy of Music to see operas. We made many trips there. We saw Aida, La Boheme, Carmen, La

Traviata and others. I can't remember all of them.

I do remember that later during World War II my brother Frank bought four tickets to the Metropolitan Opera House in Manhattan. It was the first time we went there. We saw "Lucia Di Lamamoor," and a new singer was making her debut, Patrice Munsel. She was fantastic. Visiting the Opera House was such a great experience for all of us. All the women looked beautiful the way they were dressed and the men also looked great.

My brother Frank told me about the time my Mother and Father, together with my Aunt Rosalie and Uncle Joseph bought property out on Staten Island, New York City. It was their summer getaway. They planted all kinds of vegetables and tomatoes. When the tomatoes were ripe to be picked, they would gather them and place them in the sun to dry.

The tomatoes were crushed and made into paste which was used for tomato sauce for pasta. I don't recall any of this because I was very young and I guess I stayed home with Grandma.

Moving On

It was a very happy time for me growing up at Hegney Place. Unfortunately, my folks lost the house when my Mother became sick and the bank foreclosed. By this time I was ten years old and I wasn't happy about living in an apartment house. It was never the same. However, life must go on.

When I was about eleven years old, we lived on this block, 150th Street in the Bronx. It was called Hogan's Alley. Don't know how it got the name. Anyway, my friends and I loved to skate down the street. We would have a race to see who was the fastest skater.

There was a family, the Grosso's, that lived above my

family on the third floor. The strange thing about that was that in years to come, I would marry the son, Carmine, in 1947. We would be married for 64 years when he passed away in 2011 at age 88.

While living here on 150th Street, one day I came down with a high fever. I didn't know what I had, but my folks called a doctor. He gave me some pills to swallow. I always had a problem swallowing pills, especially if they were a little bit bigger. I pretended to swallow them. I used to throw them under the bed. As a result, I wasn't getting better and the doctor and my parents couldn't understand why not. When my Father was cleaning one morning, he swept under the bed and all the pills came out. He got so mad at me because it cost money for the doctor as well as for the medicine and of course I was still very sick.

We lived on 150th Street until 1936 when my Grandmother passed away. She was 93 years old. Then we moved around the corner to Brook Avenue. It was a cold water flat. We had hot water but no steam heat. We had kerosene stoves to keep us warm. I used to sleep in the living room on a folding bed and next to my bed was one of those stoves. I was lucky we never had a fire or I wouldn't be here now. I was going to junior high school at that time.

When we lived at Brook Avenue, the cold water flat, my cousins moved in, cousin Jim and his wife Caroline and their children Jimmy, Jr. and baby Dorothy, who was 18 months old. There were boxes all over, since they just moved in the day before. It was summer time and the windows were opened. The baby was in the crib which was in the living room. Somehow the baby climbed out of the crib and got onto a box near the window. Apparently she crawled onto the window sill and fell out to the ground below. She fell five stories down, hitting the concrete. She was killed instantly. If I close my eyes I can still see her little body in the coffin. She looked like a little sleeping angel.

The family didn't bother to unpack. They moved away as soon as they could make arrangements. They were just devastated.

Here I am as a teenager

Growing up and Going to School

I did graduate from junior high school in 1939 and from high school in 1942. World War II was going on and two of my brothers were in the army. Gene, my oldest brother, was a radio man in the Air Force, and my brother Dominick was a Chef in the Infantry.

In 1942 the year I graduated from high school, I remember we were living in this apartment house. It was on 141ˢᵗ Street and Willis Avenue. There were seven rooms all off a long hallway. It was the best apartment we ever lived in. The reason I mention it is because it was the first time in my life that I had my very own room. I always slept with my Grandmother when I was young; after she died I used to sleep in the living room on a folding bed. The first night I slept in my own room, I had nightmares. I wasn't used to the darkness or being in a closed environment. I must have cried out in my sleep because my Mother came in asking me what was the matter. I guess I had a little bit of claustrophobia. I don't like being in small closed areas.

Unfortunately we didn't stay there very long. The super who lived next door to us was a madman. He used to beat up his mother. He was a big fat man and she was a little woman. Whenever he had to fix something in our apartment, he always carried a hammer in his hand, which scared my Mother. She was afraid he might get mad and hit her with it. After all, he did hit his mother.

So we moved again, this time to 138th Street near Willis Avenue.

The Telephone

We got our first telephone when we were living at 138th Street. I think it was in 1942. I recall that after World War II started and my two brothers had been drafted, we wanted to get a phone put in the apartment. We wanted it so they could call us and let us know how they were doing and where they were stationed. We got in touch with the phone company and set up an appointment for someone to come over. They had to see if there were other lines in the building. If there were, it would be easier to get a phone.

Anyway the day finally came and we got our first phone installed. It was a wall phone with a dial but no coin slots. They didn't have a table phone to give us. Next, we had to decide where to put it, so it was put on the wall in my bedroom. It was the only spot that was feasible. I didn't mind it being there at first, but later on it was a big nuisance. My brother Salvator's girlfriend, Celia, had a habit of calling him at night after she got off from work after eleven o'clock. I was trying to sleep, after all I had to go to work in the morning. He would be on the phone for an hour or more. I would yell at him to hang up so I could go back to sleep. When he finally ended his conversation he got mad at me and called me a brat.

I don't recall when the phone company called us and asked us if we wanted a table phone, to which we said, "Yes, yes!" I was so happy I finally got my bedroom to myself again.

I was married from there in 1947. That was the last place my Mother and Father lived until they died. My Father died September 8, 1958 at age 67. My Mother died December 25, 1963, she was 73 years old. Five years later on December 25, 1968, my Mother-in-law Anna passed away. She was 70 years old.

Going to Work

In 1942 when I graduated from high school, I went out into the City to find a job. I liked New York City and it was easy getting to Manhattan from the Bronx via the subway. I went into banks and insurance companies and other businesses. Being it was war time I didn't think I would have a problem getting a job. In high school I had bookkeeping, steno, "Gregg." I had learned typing in the eighth grade when I was in junior high, P.S. 30.

But getting a job wasn't easy. I began to wonder if my name had anything to do with it. I am of Italian descent, my name was Sarullo - and we were at war with Italy.

Finally in August of that year I got a job with the Corn Exchange Bank. It was a bookkeeping job. I had to learn to operate this Burrough's machine. You put in a ledger sheet with the name of the depositor, then posted the amount of the check on it. It was interesting and I learned fast. The salary wasn't tremendous, only $16.75 a week. Imagine living on that today. I didn't stay there very long.

I went to an employment agency and got a better job in a bank on Broadway and 57th Street, West Side Federal Savings & Loan Association. There I was getting $25.00 per week and there was air conditioning not like at the other bank, and I didn't have to work every Saturday. I was off every other one. They started me out as a file girl. I had to learn the switchboard. Then a new boss took me under his wing and taught me how to post the general ledger. I loved that, I always liked to work with figures, still do. As the years went by, I was in the Comptroller's Department as an assistant. I loved my job and all the people working around me. I had to, I was there for 38 years. I retired in January 1982 at age 57.

I remember when I was 22 years old, I had become very ill. I was running a temperature over 102 degrees for several days. Finally my Mother called the doctor. He examined me and told my parents that I had meningitis. My Mother became hysterical, thinking I was going to die. The doctor gave me a new antibiotic called penicillin. The shots were given in the buttocks, they were so painful. The doctor gave me three shots in the course of three days. However after a week went by and I wasn't getting any better, my Mother called in another doctor. This doctor said I didn't have meningitis, I had the grippe, which resembles influenza. With his treatment of sulfur pills, I recovered quickly. He told my Mother to feed me and give me soda to drink. The first doctor said I could not have any food, only water. I was very hungry. Anyway I finally got well and was able to go back to work.

My Brothers after World War II

My brother Gene, who was in the Army Air Force spent a lot of time in the Philippines and then New Guinea. I believe it was when he was in New Guinea that he became ill with malaria. He was very sick and it somehow damaged his heart. In 1945 he was discharged from the Army because of his medical problems.

My brother Gene in uniform with my parents

My brother Dominick in the service

Gene married his fiancee Rose that year. Years later he had two lovely daughters, Linda and Lisa. Unfortunately, due to his bad heart, he died in 1974 at age 58.

Brother Dominick was stationed mostly in the U.S. and Hawaii. He did go to Japan after the war was over, after Japan surrendered. He was discharged in1946. He also married his fiancee Angelina that year. They had two children, Vincent and Catherine. In March 2001, Dominick died at age 80 due to complications from hip surgery. His wife, Angelina died that same year in December from cancer. She was 76 years old.

My two other brothers weren't in the service, Salvator because of poor health and Frank because of poor eyesight. Salvator died in 1995, he was 77 years old. Frank is still going strong. We celebrated his 90th birthday November 19, 2012. We had a big family get together. He enjoyed the party so much, he still talks about it two years later.

My brothers Salvator and Gene

Carmine in his Navy uniform

Carmine

My brother Frank and my husband Carmine went to school together, from elementary up to six grade. Then they went to Clark Junior High School. In those days they had what they called the Rapids in junior high. Before you graduated from sixth grade everyone took a test to see if they would get into the Rapids. For students who were smarter they would get to finish junior high in a year and a half instead of three years, 7th, 8th and 9th grades. Carmine was one of the boys who made the Rapids. Also I thought you would like to know that Carmine was the only boy who passed the test to get into Stuyvesant High School in Manhattan out of 500 students in Clark Junior High.

Carmine's father, John, worked as a blaster. He worked building subway tunnels and also was in charge of building the Empire State Building. He was the person in charge of the blasting powder, how much to use and when. They had to dig a deep foundation for that building. Because they didn't have protective gear in those days, John became sick with lung disease. John was a young man with a wife and three children, Dominick, Carmine and Margaret. John died when he was only 40 years old as a result of his illness. Carmine was only 16 years old.

The oldest son, Dominick, died in June 1950 from kidney disease, he was only 28 years old. The only daughter, Margaret, died October 19, 1996 from cancer. She was 71 years old.

Dominick was married to Antoinette. They had two children, Anne and John. Margaret was married to Gino. They had three children, Gina, John and Michael.

Carmine's First Marriage and the Birth of Lois Ann

My brother Frank was best man at Carmine's and Louise's wedding in 1942. Carmine was home on leave from the Navy and he wanted to get married. His family was against it because they thought he was too young, only 19 years old. So Carmine and Louise eloped. After they were married they went back to his base in Illinois. He was going to Hospital Corps School in Great Lakes, Illinois. He completed the course July 2, 1943. When Louise became pregnant she didn't want to have her baby there. She wanted to go back to New York to be close to her family, particularly her mother. Unfortunately things went very badly during delivery. Louise died after delivering a beautiful and healthy baby girl, Lois.

Carmine was in the Navy. He enlisted when war broke out, he didn't want to go into the Army. He always wanted to be a doctor, so he applied for the Medical Division and he became a Pharmacist's Assistant. Whenever they had shore leave, it was his job to check the sailors out, to make sure that they didn't bring back any diseases. They were on a small ship, it was an L.S.T. (which stands for "Landing Ship, Tank," a flat bottom boat.)

During World War II when Carmine was in the Navy he was in the Pacific. His L.S.T. ship was carrying ammunition to supply other ships. At one point they were hit with a torpedo from a Japanese submarine. Luckily it was not a direct hit or they would have all been killed. Carmine was hurt but not seriously. He was entitled to the Purple Heart medal but he never wanted to apply for it.

There was an incident when a young sailor became sick and they had to operate aboard ship. They had to do an appendectomy. Carmine assisted the doctor. When the war was coming to an end, Carmine had become Chief Pharmacist Mate. Navy personnel wanted him to stay in the

Navy and continue his education in medical school. I wish he had, that was his first love, to be a doctor. The reason he wanted to leave was because he had a little girl at home, hadn't seen her since she was a baby. He never became a doctor, going back to school was difficult after four years in the Navy. He was honorably discharged in January 1946.

Carmine and I

In January 1946, after both my brothers were home from the war, we had a big "Welcome Home" party for them. We invited many people, relatives and friends. My brother Frank invited Carmine to the party. It was the first time I saw him since he came home from the Navy. A neighbor of ours asked me about Carmine, if he was married or single. "He is so handsome," she said, "he would make a good catch for me." I told her I wasn't interested in him, he was just Frank's friend.

It was in the springtime of that year when I became sick and the doctor said I had meningitis. My brother went to see Carmine to ask him about this disease. As I mentioned earlier, Carmine was a Chief Pharmacist Mate in the Navy. Carmine told Frank that they usually do a spinal tap to determine if it is meningitis. A few days later Carmine came to my house and brought me a box of candy. He did so at his mother's insistence.

During this time he and my brother would go out for a ride in his car. I never did, I wasn't asked. However, as time went on Carmine asked me if I would like to go for a ride and I said sure. Thus started our courtship. First it was with Frank and then my other brother Dominick and his wife Ann came along with us too. So in the beginning Carmine came along with our family on picnics and other outings.

This is me at Easter time before I was married

Carmine said he was tired of chasing after me, I was too aloof. Eventually it became only a twosome, him and me.

We were engaged November of that year and married on May 25, 1947.

This is my wedding dress that my mother made out of one of the two silk parachutes that my brother Dominick brought back from Japan.

Married Life

Carmine and I were married three months before my 23rd birthday (August 23) and two months before his 24th (July 15) and 16 days before his little girl Lois's third birthday, June 10. We were married in Saint Jerome's Church at 138th Street and Alexander Avenue in the Bronx. It was such a beautiful church.

My Mother was a seamstress, as I mentioned earlier. So when I made plans for my wedding, she made my dress. She made it out of one of the two silk parachutes that my brother Dominick brought back from Japan. The previous year, when Dominick and Angelina got married, my Mom also made her gown from one of the parachutes. On my gown she sewed sequins on the bodice and down the sides of the dress and on to the train. It was beautiful. It took her three months to make it. I wanted to save it, but it was

My mother with my Sister-in-law, Angela, working on Angela's wedding dress. This dress was also made from a silk parachute.

ruined because of a leak in the ceiling. Everything in the closet got soaked. It broke my heart to throw the dress away.

When Carmine and I got married we went down to South Carolina for our honeymoon, a town called Fountain Inn. His uncle and aunt lived there, they met during the war. She was a nurse in the Army and he was a soldier. He was wounded and she took care of him, that's how they met. Anyway, we didn't stay at their house. Instead, we went to stay at Mrs. Hoffman's house. It was a beautiful colonial house. Every morning she would bring up a tray of coffee and cream and freshly made biscuits, they were so good.

I want to mention that we went down to South Carolina by train and we had our own compartment. I think they called it a drawing room. The steward came in at night to make up our bed. It was pure luxury riding that way. On our return trip a week later, we came home by plane, the first time for me. I enjoyed that immensely. I forgot to mention that when we were in Fountain Inn, we visited many points of interest in North and South Carolina, including trips through the Blue Ridge Mountains and parts of the Great Smokey Range. That was in 1947. We did go back again in 1949.

In August 1947, we got this apartment on 174th Street and Boone Avenue in the Bronx. It was a walk up and we got the apartment on the fifth floor. It was nice, one bedroom, small kitchen and a good size living room, bathroom and a nice foyer. I remember that in the summer it was very hot and in the winter it was very cold. The first year we didn't have a fan, however we did buy two the next summer. The reason we were so cold in the winter was that our windows faced the 174th Street Bridge, it was all open space.

That year was a bad winter, we had a lot of snow. The

day after Christmas we got twenty-four inches of snow, nothing moved. We couldn't go to work. A few days later my husband and I were walking to the 174th Street train station. As we were walking, we had to go downhill. Somehow my husband slipped, there must have been ice under the snow. He fell down hitting his head hard on the ground. He said he was alright, so we went on to the train. My job was on West 57th Street and his was on West 125th Street. A few days later when he woke up he said he had double vision. He couldn't stand up or walk. I had to get help so I could get him to a doctor. My regular doctor suggested that I take him to a neurologist. He recommended one and I took Carmine there. After a thorough examination the neurologist said it wasn't anything serious and all Carmine needed was bed rest. It took several weeks before the double vision went away. He was as good as new after that.

Where we were living we were within walking distance of the Bronx Park Zoo. We would go there many times in the evenings and also on weekends. I took Lois Ann and my super's little girl, Mary, to the park on Saturdays. They had a great time. I put them on the animal rides and bought them toys and food.

When Carmine and I were married over a year, we wanted to take Lois Ann to live with us. From the time she was nine days old she had been living with my Mother-in-law and Sister-in-law. I told Carmine that Lois Ann should be living with us – he was her father and I wanted to be her Mother. However, things got heated up with his Mother and other family members, that it was cruel and heartless to take her away from the only mother she knew. So my husband gave in and Lois Ann grew up in Grandma's house.

February 1956 we moved from our 174th Street apartment into a two family house on Wallace Avenue. We had the upstairs apartment. It had four rooms – two bedrooms, a good size living room and a very large kitchen. Also there was a large walk-in cupboard in the kitchen. It was great for all my dishes and pots and pans and foodstuff. The bedroom had four windows. One was a bay window with three windows and then there was one window on the other side. I did a beautiful job draping all the windows. We liked it there the first year. The landlady and her mother were very friendly and they gave us vegetables and tomatoes from their garden. That was the first year.

The second winter, 1957, things changed. Our apartment was very cold, so I complained about it. The landlady said I should wear more clothes, don't walk around in your nightgown. I said to her that how I walked around dressed had nothing to do with the lack of heat. It was so cold in the bedroom we had to take the mattress and put it on the floor in the middle room. It became our refrigerator where we kept our potatoes and onions and even wine. The temperature was as low as 40°. How we survived is beyond me.

She also complained that I took too long doing my dishes, wasted too much water and that we made too much noise. We were only two people and we went out to work every day, out before 7 am. and home after 6 pm. I believe the lady was a bit crazy. She accused me of dirtying her windows. I said to her "How could I do that? I can't reach your windows."

Finally we moved out, February 1958. We rented an apartment in Westchester County on Bronx River Road. That year we bought a Volkswagen, the bug. It was fun riding in that car, the sloping hood brought the road closer.

Our Trips and Vacations

Carmine liked to go fishing and hunting. He showed me how to put a worm on the hook. I didn't care for that, too slimy. His famous place to fish was out on Long Island, Shinnecock Bay. We would rent a row boat and row out to a spot, drop anchor and fish. The best fishing was during fluke season. They were so good pan fried. When he went hunting with the guys I sometimes went with him. I learned how to shoot a .22 gauge rifle and also a .20 gauge shotgun. I never killed anything, I liked to target shoot best of all. One year we went hunting for bear up in Bangor, Maine, but we didn't come across any. I was glad about that, only saw a red fox.

September, 1950 my husband and I went on vacation to Canada. We toured the City of Quebec. Carmine took French in high school and also in college. Therefore he was able to speak to the waiters or waitresses when we ordered our meals.

After Quebec we went to the Laurentian Mountains and stayed at a great resort for a week. It was a popular resort in the winter. Unfortunately, I can't remember the name. On another vacation we went up to the Pocono Mountains and stayed there for a week. We did a lot of fishing and touring the countryside. We also went to the Amish Country, that was very interesting and the food was great.

We also spent a lot of time on Long Island. I remember that the summer of 1958 we first rented a cabin in Long Island. Therefore we had to bring our pots and pans and linens out to the cabin. It was very funny, we loaded the Volksie with all the stuff and the three of us! Carmine and I in the front and poor Lois in the back. She barely had room to move. However, we had a great time.

We stayed at the summer cottage for our two week vacation a couple of times. It was in Hampton Bay. We would got out to Oscar's in Shinnecock Bay, rent a boat and go fishing. Whatever fish we caught there was someone at the boathouse who would clean and fillet the fish, so all we had to do was cook them when we got back at the cottage.

I Learn to Drive

When I was about 50 years old I decided I wanted to learn how to drive. My brothers never wanted to teach me and neither did my husband. So I called a driving school in Manhattan. I used to work at 1790 Broadway. On the very first day I had my lesson, the instructor told me to get behind the wheel. I was petrified, I said to him, "this is such a busy area." "Don't worry," he said, "you will be fine." So I took the wheel and started to drive.

I drove across 57th Street to the Eastside. I went up to East 125th Street. After my lesson was over I got off at 125th Street and took the Metro North train home to Yonkers. I took several more lessons in the City. Then I got in touch with an instructor in Yonkers. This time I had a woman, I think her name was Judy. She was very good. I learned so much from her. When the time came for me to take my driving test, she was there with me. I did very well. I wasn't nervous, though I thought I would be. I passed on the first try.

The reason I was anxious to learn how to drive was because Carmine was away very often. He was working in Connecticut. He went on Monday morning and didn't return until Friday evening. So I was alone a lot. Our car was sitting in the parking lot. I walked to the supermarket and all other stores. When I finally got my license I was able to drive on my own. What a great feeling that was – freedom to drive yourself wherever you wanted to go. Utter independence.

Carmine and I in Our Later Years

Due to the fact that Carmine and I grew up during the Depression era, we agreed that we would not end up like our parents with no money in our old age. We both worked and so it was easy for us to put a little money in a savings account every payday. When we accumulated a good sum, we invested in C.D's (certificates of deposit). We kept doing this over and over taking advantage of the high interest rates over the years. At one point we were getting 12% on C.D.'s for five years.

Back in 2010 my husband and I moved from Yonkers where we had lived for 53 years, to a retirement residence. It was called "Cedar Crest" in Pompton Plains, New Jersey. I thought it would be a good place for my husband because he had Parkinson's Disease. They told me he would get special exercises and that he would be with other afflicted men and

Photo: Asher Susswein

My husband Carmine, myself and my brother Frank

women. He only got around in a wheelchair which was pushed by the aide I hired to help him. We had a nice apartment, two bedrooms, kitchen, living room and dining area. It was nice, but expensive. We could go down to the restaurant for dinner or we could eat in our apartment. Food wasn't so good, many times the meat was tough. My husband had trouble eating it.

I didn't find people to be very friendly. Needless to say, I wasn't happy there and neither was my husband. We moved back to Yonkers in May 2011 after seven months at Cedar Crest. Unfortunately my husband wasn't getting any better, he deteriorated rapidly and died on November 4, 2011.

Lois, my Grandchildren and Great-Grandchildren

As a child Lois Ann went to a Catholic School, The Immaculate Conception elementary school. When she graduated from there she went to St. Barnabas High School in Yonkers. She was a very smart and beautiful young woman. We wanted her to go to college, but she fell in love with a handsome young man and wanted to get married. We were unhappy about this because she was so young. We wanted her to spread her wings and see the world.

Lois and Raymond did get married, eventually. They had three beautiful boys. Raymond Jr., the oldest, went to Rutgers University, specializing in Electrical Engineering and got his degree. Today he is a professional engineer. Ronald, the second son, also went to Rutgers. He always wanted to be a Doctor since he was a little boy. That is what he is today, an ear, nose and throat doctor. Robert the youngest son is a professional video engineer and doing very well. Raymond has two older daughters from when he was married to his first wife, Charlotte. Danielle now twenty-six years old and Victoria age twenty-three years. He also has lovely twin girls with his second wife, Asavari. The girls names are Jasmin and Mia age ten years old. They were eleven November 8, 2014.

Ronald is married to Allison, his second wife. They have two beautiful little girls, Miranda age eight and Adrienne age seven.

Robert is married to Maria. They have a beautiful little son, Robbie, Jr. He was six on October 21, 2014.

My daughter Lois divorced her first husband because he was a very abusive man to her and to the children. He owned a dry cleaning business. When things didn't go well at work he would brood about it and take it out on Lois and the boys.

Years later she married Tony, her second husband. Tony worked with the singer/actor David Bowie, he was Bowie's bodyguard. Wherever Bowie went Tony traveled with him. As a result my daughter and the boys went with him. They traveled to many parts of the world – Australia,

Japan, France and England. They lived in England for awhile. They also toured most of the American West. Tony was very good to her and helped with raising the boys.

Lois was a great Mother, a bit strict, but very loving. She would do anything for her kids. She is also a very loving Grandmother to all of her six granddaughters and one grandson.

My daughter is now married to Richard, a wonderful and loving man. Richard is very good to me. He makes sure that I get to the gym and to the senior center on time. He drops me off and then picks me up when I'm finished. He does everything to make sure that I'm happy. I love him like a son. I love my daughter very much, she does so much for me. She also drives me to the gym and the senior center classes.

New Beginnings

After my husband passed away I was living alone in my Yonkers apartment house. My daughter and her husband, Rick, thought it would be best if I moved in with them. Her townhouse was too small, so we had a new house built with a special area for me. My new quarters consisted of a sitting room, a large bedroom and my own bathroom. It was really great, and I didn't have any stairs to climb to get to it. I lived there for over one year and I like it very much. I joined the gym, I went twice a week and to the senior center one day a week. What I liked about the senior center was that we went on trips. I went on a nine day trip to Branson, Missouri and I enjoyed that very much. Not bad for a ninety year old.

On the week of my birthday, August 23, my grandson Ronnie and his family surprised me when they came up from Georgia to celebrate my special day, my ninetieth birthday.

It was the best birthday ever. The other two grandsons were away on vacation.

On December 11, 2014, the Woodbury Senior Center where I was a member had a Christmas Party for us at the Falkirk Country Club. It was a great party, good food and music, many were dancing, even me. The best part is all the wonderful people and they are so friendly. I just loved it.

I liked living here in Woodbury Junction. All the great friends I made at the Woodbury Senior Center and Golden Age Club. I will miss them all very much.

We are moving to Georgia.

On September 3, 2015, we did move into our new home in Alpharetta, Georgia. It is a lovely home, has many windows. It's an older house, not a brand new one like our last home. The area is beautiful, trees all around, well-kept grounds, great roads. So far people seem to be very friendly. As soon as we get a bit settled, I will see about getting to the

Senior Center . I hope to remain here for the rest of my life.

Looking Back and Looking Forward

The biggest regret of my life is that I didn't fight harder to take Lois Ann away from her Grandmother and come live with her father Carmine and me. I also regret that I wasn't closer to her while she was growing up, like a real Mom should have been.

The other thing I regret is not traveling after we retired. My husband didn't want to go anywhere, he just wanted to stay home. We had the means to travel, but we didn't.

A couple of years ago I reunited with my cousins in California. Haven't seen cousin Jimmy since he was eleven years old and I was fifteen. Cousin Robert and cousin Jean I never met. However, we keep in touch by telephone. I wanted to take a trip out there, but I couldn't travel by myself.

Christmas time, December 24th 2014 brought to mind when I was little. On Christmas Eve we would eat at the regular time. We had all kinds of fish and spaghetti with baccala. Then at midnight my Mom and aunts would start cooking all the meat. Sausage and peppers and veal cutlets, potatoes and vegetables. Real good stuff. Then we all sat around the table and started to eat again.

Those were good times. These are good times. There are good times still to come.

Ciao!

ACKNOWLEDGMENT

My sincere thanks to my niece, Linda. She spent many hours editing my writing, correcting my grammar and shortening my long sentences.

Back Cover Photo: Asher Susswein

Made in the USA
Columbia, SC
13 September 2017